The Racial Healing Handbook

Why we have to talk About Racism, Multicultural Society and Solve the Cynical Mind-set that Plagues America. A Book About White Privilege, White Rage and Black Dignity.

Timothy Diakité

© **Copyright 2019 - All rights reserved.**

The content contained within this book may not be reproduced, duplicated or transmitted without direct written permission from the author or the publisher.

Under no circumstances will any blame or legal responsibility be held against the publisher, or author, for any damages, reparation, or monetary loss due to the information contained within this book, either directly or indirectly.

Legal Notice:

This book is copyright protected. It is only for personal use. You cannot amend, distribute, sell, use, quote or paraphrase any part, or the content within this book, without the consent of the author or publisher.

Disclaimer Notice:

Please note the information contained within this document is for educational and entertainment purposes only. All effort has been executed to present accurate, up to date, reliable, complete information. No warranties of any kind are declared or implied. Readers acknowledge that the author is not engaged in the rendering of legal, financial, medical or professional advice.

The content within this book has been derived from various sources. Please consult a licensed professional before attempting any techniques outlined in this book.

By reading this document, the reader agrees that under no circumstances is the author responsible for any losses, direct or indirect, that are incurred as a result of the use of the information contained within this document, including, but not limited to, errors, omissions, or inaccuracies.

Table of Contents

Introduction..5

Chapter 1..4

Beginning of Racist Ideas in America

Chapter 2..8

Different Faces of Racism

Chapter 3..25

Exploring White Privilege

Chapter 4..30

Where Does White Rage Come From?

Chapter 5..36

Why Racism is a Threat to All of Us

Chapter 6..44

Psychology of Racism and its Poisonous Consequences

Chapter 7..71

How to Deal with Racism

Chapter 8..82

How to Deal with the Toxic Mind-sets & Change Them

Chapter 9..92

How to Reorient Conversations About Racism

Chapter 10..101

Combatting Racism

Chapter 11..111

Beyond the Awareness of Racism & Becoming an Anti-Racist

Chapter 12..121

How to Teach Your Children About Racism

Chapter 13..131

Necessity of Diversity

Introduction

"No one is born hating another person because of the colour of his skin, or his background, or his religion. People must learn to hate, and if they can learn to hate, they can be taught to love, for love comes more naturally to the human heart than its opposite."

Nelson Mandela

"The function, the very serious function of racism is distraction. It keeps you from doing your work. It keeps you explaining, over and over again, your reason for being."

Toni Morrison

"Rivers do not drink their own water; trees do not eat their own fruit; the sun does not shine on itself and flowers do not spread their fragrance for themselves. Living for others is a rule of nature. We are all born to help each other. No matter how difficult it is. Life is good when you are happy; but much better when others are happy because of you."

Pope Francis

The above quotes you have just read – from Nobel Peace Prize recipient, Nelson Mandela, former president of South Africa – Pulitzer Prize and Nobel Literature Prize recipient, US-born Toni Morrison, and Latin American-born Pope Francis, are well and truly quite profound.

It was thought that it would be appropriate to include these famous quotes on countering racism in our midst at the beginning of this book Racism & White Fragility. It might also be auspicious in the sense that around the time the book was being drafted, it was the birthday anniversary of the South African legend.

Who better to listen to and read on racism and its consequences, and how to counter it in your lives. It is also a time when racism has reared its ugly head once more. All across America, the fires are raging and the iconic hashtag that is Black Lives Matter searches for new feeds all across the world.

But at the same time, there are those who wish to argue that while black lives matter – that they do at this point in humanity's history cannot be doubted or even question - all lives matter rather. Indeed, in a perfect world, that much is true.

But unfortunately, this is not a perfect world and whilst socio- economic and democratic progress has been made all across the world, it has not been enough. Those who profess to the credo that 'all lives matter' may merely be augmenting their ulterior motives in the sense that white lives matter more.

Certainly, not just in America, there are hidden agendas all across the planet, but as Lori-Anne Johnson, a senior health professional in the UK has remarked; while black people at large remain amongst the most marginalized and oppressed, the spirited fight must go on.

In South Africa, during the concerted and violent struggles against an inherently oppressive regime there was this iconic mantra;

Aluta Continua

But perhaps even Mr. Mandela would beg to differ. Because it was he, after twenty-seven years of incarceration under the racist regime of South Africa, who preached the message of reconciliation rather than prolonging this country's unique racial conflicts. Now that he has passed, Black Economic Empowerment remains alive and well in South Africa.

And the struggle continues.

And so it goes that it is the most marginalized and oppressed of South Africa's society, not just black but white as well, that continue to bear the brunt. Something has got to give, surely. When does it end? And where to begin? With hope? Well, why not then?

Let's begin this narrative with Hawaiian-born Barack Obama. This is a gentleman who needs very little introduction. After all, he was the first black or African-American citizen to be elected to the USA's highest office.

He successfully completed a second term of office as President of the United States of America, purportedly 'the land of the free and the home of the brave', after fending off his formidable Republican opponent, Mormon billionaire Mitt Romney. He won the Noble Peace Prize and today many people still wonder why. Today still, Mr. Obama is still a strong advocate of affirmative action in lieu of aiding this country's racial minorities to achieve equality across the board.

In terms of addressing minority concerns in the Republic of South Africa, is unfortunately quite another matter.

The reader must remember that whilst these two remarkable countries tragically share much in common in regard to racial oppression across the centuries since the first white settlers arrived, their circumstances are dissimilar.

But in an effort to seek academic, economic, psychological, spiritual, religious, as well as political solutions to end racism, institutionalized or otherwise, for once and for all, it could prove to be an enriching experience in contrasting the paths of these two great countries.

But in view of the global attention that the USA has attracted, it is necessary to focus on this country for now. And at the time of writing, the Statue of Liberty was still standing.

Today, in America, as well as South Africa, and for that matter, many parts of the world, the oppression of minorities is not only racially motivated. They are gender-based as well.

And yet still, it was Mr. Obama who crossly remarked that he was not elected President of the Harvard Law Society through affirmative action but on his own terms. Indeed, this much is true.

But could it be argued that his meritorious achievements would not have been possible had it not been for the sacrifices made by the likes of Martin Luther King who had a dream and Malcolm X who rolled up his sleeves to take on racism by any means necessary.

And, for that matter, Nelson Mandela, arguable the world's most beloved icon since both World War Two hero, Winston Churchill, and the universal scion for world peace and equality in all its manifestations, Mahatma K Ghandi.

All this book seeks to do is to play its part in helping to reverse the ineptitude of crass racism, racism and discrimination in all its forms. But in order to do so, it needs to go back in history because at some point, this is where racial conflict started.

One clear example of this may well be the US Civil War. Today, there are those who believe that Republican President Abraham Lincoln waged war against the Confederates on behalf of the black slaves. It turns out that it was nothing of the sort. As former US President Bill Clinton remarked; it's the economy, stupid.

About this Book

The book begins with the origins of themes of racial supremacy and its ideologies. The beginning of racist thought could be closely

aligned with the prevailing tendencies of white privilege while at the same time wonder where past and current white rage emanates.

Those who wish to argue that black rage is prevalent in our societies as well need to be reminded once more that it remains the case that black people at large remain on the margins of society and, in particular women and children, are most oppressed.

The issue to hand is to explore ways of overcoming this rage for once and for all. After all, it was Mandela who said that if a child can be taught to hate, it could be taught to love as well. The first exploratory chapter deals with the warning of why racism remains so threatening.

It then explores the psychological aspects of racism while noting its consequences. A demonstration is presented on how racism indoctrinates to the detriment of the affected individual's self-worth. A return to history is made by studying institutionalized racism in America. It might also be worthwhile at this point to compare it with the epicenter of institutionalized racism, apartheid South Africa.

And then let the healing begin.

Following chapters present ideas on how to deal with racism, counter it through the peaceful, non-violent means of transforming conversations in and around racism. Ignorance of racism must surely also be addressed. While learning how to become an anti-racism advocate you could and perhaps should, also be teaching your young children.

To close the book, one final argument is put forward. The need for diversity.

Chapter 1

Beginning of Racist Ideas in America

This chapter will briefly account the ominous beginnings of racism in America. But at the same time, it can record successful revolts.

Since its first colonizers arrived from Europe, mainly from Spain, France and the British Empire, the US has always been an import- oriented nation.

And while it is well-known that this country imported its first slaves from Africa, it imported racial and/or racist ideologies and philosophies as well.

The earliest journal entry records that a handful of Angolan slaves were transported by Portuguese traders to be disembarked on the quayside of then British Virginia.

But the manifestation of racial prejudice and oppression goes back further to the fifteenth century around the time the hapless explorer Christopher Columbus discovered the Americas. His fellow travelers may not have transported slaves but certainly made slaves of America's indigenous tribes.

Perhaps the highlight of racial ideologies and its inherent enslavement of 'non-white' peoples had its origins around the time of the so-called Cotton Wars to the closing stanzas of the Civil War. Indeed, it was Abraham Lincoln, as Commander in Chief, who misled black conscripts and volunteers because after Lincoln was assassinated the black settlers never received their promised freedom.

But to return to America's War for Independence, it could very well be argued that racial ideology was formally declared when Thomas Jefferson lifted aspects of philosopher Thomas Aquina's thoughts on equality and freedom to declare the Constitution of the United States of America a legal and binding document in the 'universal' pursuit of happiness.

Alongside of the country's early years of enforced and institutionalized racism, came the first revolts. Today's Black Lives

Matter campaign is nothing new and indeed it does pale into insignificance in the sense that Nat Turner's campaign, thirty years before the US Civil War, was successful.

And of course, there have been many more anti-racism campaigns since then, many of them violent but some of them peaceful. Perhaps the most famous statements of intent by peaceful means was made during the Montgomery Bus Boycott and the Selma to Montgomery March, led by Nobel Peace Prize recipient Martin Luther King.

What were they marching for and against? It was in the post-war years of the twentieth century that racial segregation was fomented coincidentally in the years during which South Africa's Nationalist (white) government tightened its grip on the majority by introducing a raft of racist laws.

Now, what stands out in the abovementioned marches against racial oppression, institutionalised or otherwise? The fact of the matter remains that these marches by thousands of people were peaceful in the main. Indeed, Dr Martin Luther King was a disciple of the Mahatma's satyagraha (civil disobedience, or rather; insistence, holding firmly to, holding onto truth) philosophies. So too fellow Peace Prize recipient Albert Luthuli of South Africa.

And in later years, Nelson Mandela.

Chapter 2

Different Faces of Racism

Inasmuch as the mirror has two faces, so it goes that racism, in all its ugliness, it turns out, has many faces.

How is this possible? This chapter will explore this briefly. It also seeks to counter the myth that racial oppression lies at the hands of white majorities (or minorities) who currently hold the levers of power, whether through democratic means or even through coercion.

It has to be said further that so-called voter apathy – in terms of not going to the polls to vote for new representatives – could be a guilty party in playing the race card.

The perception remains. What is the point of voting within the status quo when it is inherently upholding a racist regime? Perhaps there are those who have short memories because was it twelve years ago at the time of publishing this book that Hawaiian-born Barack

Obama, of Kenyan (African) descent became the first African- American or black President of the United States of America.

And after he stepped down after completing two successful terms of office during which he laid down the law in terms of achieving equality across the board, not just in terms of racial redress, did he not also achieve important milestones.

His White House was by and large a representative one. This is contrary to popular belief. And not only the inclusion of African- American and Hispanic minorities but a transgendered citizen as well.

And was it not true that during the presidential election prior to Mr. Obama laying down the wreaths of power, Senator Hilary Clinton was on the verge of making history once more by becoming this country's first female President.

By and large, she won the popular vote. And so it went that Republican candidate Donald Trump sneaked into the White House by way of the country's, many would believe (and this may also explain the voter apathy) skewered electoral college vote whereby a number of states, irrespective of its size and demographics but rather through historical (racist?) legacies, have influence over who should inevitably be the country's commander in chief.

Historical Overview

As noted during the introduction of this book, racism, whether institutionialised or spontaneous, was alive and well ever since the first white settlers arrived. But it needs to be made quite clear that not only did black or African-Americans bear the brunt of racism since the Declaration of Independence was made.

Indeed, the Hispanic or Latin American populace or indigenous tribes were its earliest recipients, so too the country's Native Americans, otherwise (racially) referred to as 'Indians'. Particularly at the turn of the twentieth century during which time migration from the Old Continent to the New appeared to be at a peak, further racial oppression was meted out against myriad minorities in the form of Italians, Irish, Poles and, in particular, Jews.

And in later years, particularly during and after the previous century's two world wars, Jews would come to be classed as Middle Eastern 'citizens' alongside of Arabs and Iranians to the point that they were no longer classified as 'white'.

Tragically, the crimes against humanity in the form of racial discrimination, forced removals and even genocide were not only laid against the Native Americans but also against East, South and Southeast Asians when the country 'went to war' in the interests of 'freedom and democracy'. For this the reader need look no further than the Korean and Vietnam war years overseen by no less than five US Presidents.

Structural Racism

Today, in the ongoing pursuit of happiness, structural racism continues to elude or challenge the country's racial minorities. It remains difficult for them to access decent education and jobs, proper housing and healthcare, as well as equal treatment within the criminal justice system.

But even should they be permitted to public and private institutions across the board, it remains challenging for the country's minorities to 'fit in'. There are reasons for this.

Several factors have been identified by academic scholars who have based their findings on years of research. Amongst these factors that lead to structural racism are the following.

Collectively, the racial (white) majority has been known to organize themselves in accordance with their established loyalties, factions, as well as competition amongst in-group rivals, leaving little room for those already marginalized, still looking in from the outside.

The scholars found that the tribal instinct to huddle into closed groupings has contributed towards the hardening of racist beliefs, preferences and perhaps most importantly; perceptions.

There could also be the sad reality that the racial (racist?) mindset has been passed down from generation to generation in the sense that white majorities continue to jealously guard what they have accumulated over the years, whether it's material or intellectual.

There has also been the history of segregation which still leads to people racially familiar preferring to remain aloof from all others.

Over the years, racial stereotyping has played a negative part. For instance, there is the perception of black youths who may be loitering within or wondering through a white neighborhood being perceived as criminals or likely to commit a crime.

They are thus regarded with suspicion and that tragically further foments mistrust between the races. Finally, racial stereotyping continues to play itself negatively within the media and communications industry, something from which the country's film and television industry remains famously, or notoriously known.

For instance, when black nominees are not awarded with the highest prizes at the annual Golden Globes and Academy Awards presentations, even when eventual winners are indeed worthy on merit, final outcomes are always regarded with suspicions of racial favoritism and even objected to with political motivations.

Chapter 3

Exploring White Privilege

Introduction

By dint of the chapter's name, this is an exploratory one. Three critical questions are being asked here. But there is one that needs to be responded to in order to understand and appreciate what white privilege entails.

But could this chapter begin by asking a mature question? In order to both counter and reverse white privilege in our midst, would it really help matters if you, particularly if you identify yourself as a black citizen, are antagonistic towards this phenomenon of white privilege?

Perhaps the best way to answer this question is to briefly examine the current antagonist trends. And would a useful starting point be that of examining the now-iconic hashtag, now often regurgitated, known as Black Lives Matter?

What is White Privilege?

To put it as bluntly as possible, white privilege is basically a form of social privilege that strictly benefits the white sectors of class society over others who are classed or identify as non-white (Black, African-American, Hispanic, Native American).

The tendency towards privilege sees the white majority of the country benefiting in pretty much all walks of life, namely economic, political and social. As will have been identified in an earlier chapter, white privilege in America is rooted in history, going all the way back to the time the first white settlers or colonizers arrived.

In critical race theory, one scholar has defined white privilege in Western societies at large as a litany of entitlement that was never really earned in the first instance.

Black Antagonism towards White Privilege

It has been said, generally speaking, that white people at large are at pains to understand the levels of antagonism directed towards them. After all, they believe that they are not inherently racist in the sense that they will not utilize derogatory language and may even welcome black people into their social circles.

But a salient point has been made that whilst black people and, for that matter, all other racial minorities remain on the margins of society, verbal and physical action must continue, particularly when legislative actions are laggard at best.

Indeed, one scholarly and yet, Afro-centric argument goes that whilst sectors of black people antagonize against the status quo they are not themselves racist as has been suggested by sectors of white society.

And indeed, is it not true that the current Black Lives Matter campaign continues, people from all walks of life who are not necessarily marginalized are now joining the campaign against both institutionalized and structural racism.

Can White Privilege Be Countered?

This and the concluding section of this exploratory chapter on white privilege yields optimistic responses, so do brace yourself.

Both these sections have adopted two scholarly approaches being taken towards both countering and overcoming white privilege, never mind racism itself.

The first scholarly approach argues that in order to begin to be able to counter white privilege it must be done from the vantage point of awareness as opposed to ignorance. On that same token, awareness also needs to be qualified.

And in being able to utter qualified statements or arguments, the addressee is surely able to dominate a conversation or group

discussion. But not only does this require knowledge, it also requires persistence and practice.

Having said that, could it also be a case of practicing what you preach because the argument goes further in recognizing that there may well be diverse, let alone, opposing responses towards suggestions or statements made.

Can White Privilege Be Overcome?

Speaking of practicing what one preaches, this second scholarly observation could be a case in point. It could also be a case of actions speaking louder than words. Read on then.

It is pleasing to note that white categories of society are taking conscionable action. Rather than polarize the current Black Lives Matter campaign there are concerted efforts alignments as opposed to forming more vocal alliances.

One such example is that of Showing Up for Racial Justice. This is an organization that complements the BLM campaign. It identifies as an anti-racist movement that seeks to work separately from atypical black liberation movements. The objective has been to create safe havens within which black leadership and its followings can flourish.

Chapter 4

Where Does White Rage Come From?

Introduction

It should go without saying that at some point, the conceptualized phenomenon of white rage has a beginning. At what point it comes to an end could be a talking point in later chapters of this book. For now though, let there be no confusion with Carol Anderson's bestselling book of the same title.

In order to appreciate its origins, a definition of white rage must be provided. After summarizing historical accounts of this phenomenon, this article closes on a somber note by reflecting on how white rage continues to manifest itself today.

Definition of White Rage

The localized definition of white rage in this instance refers to that of white Americans, particularly American men. In their outrage against minorities at large, theirs is typically vented against Black or African Americans.

But their rage stretches further towards other racial minorities such as Hispanic communities and migrant communities, predominantly of Asian descent.

The psychological understanding of this rage is believed to be as a consequence of being the dominant race group in the country. The rage extends further to stereotypical images or impressions of white American men in the media.

White Rage not centered on Black Minorities

But white rage is not solely focused towards racial minorities. Critically, it is focused towards those who openly or stereotypically identify with the broad-based LGBTQ communities. In this case, it can be expressed under the guise of Christian or right-wing fundamentalism. And further still, albeit in much smaller numbers, white rage could extend towards those who are classified as physically disabled or challenged.

And sadly, the prejudice towards those who are physically disabled, lesbian, gay, transsexual and/or queer comes from the racial minorities as well. It could further be argued that the rage expressed disguises own suppression as a gay or bisexual man who fears revealing his true identity.

Carol Anderson's argument on Structural Racism

Carol Anderson, as a professor in African-American studies, provides qualified theses in her studies of structural racism stretching into white rage.

The foundations of her book of the same title began in the aftermath of the Ferguson outrage on the side of black minorities. She went on to explain in a leading newspaper that this rage was in reaction to the white rage expressed against social and race-based reforms overseen by the then Obama administration.

In essence, Anderson's original mission was to 'out' white rage. She further explains that the rage has been structural all along within the country's courts and legislative institutions. Finally, the argument goes that there is resistance across the board against all forms of social advancement, particularly Black advancement.

Examining the Historical Backlash

The study takes the reader all the way back to the Jim Crow movement reacting to the end of the US Civil War and subsequent reconstruction eras. She further highlights the white backlash to various Supreme Court rulings during the nineteen-sixties.

During the Reconstruction years post-Civil war, it needs to be noted that then President Andrew Jackson was opposed to enfranchising black Americans or freed slaves.

White Rage's Violent Manifestations

The violent manifestations of white rage also have its roots in history. Wide institutionalized racism, arguably the most famous example of this was through the Klu Klux Klan movement during the second-half of the nineteenth century. This cultic tradition would go on to continue well into the twentieth century.

Today the most infamous examples of physical rage can be found in the wanton behaviour of law enforcement agents who exercised little to no restraint when apprehending black suspects of felonies however minor or major.

Alongside of this, pro-white or conservative news publications have selectively highlighted incidents of looting and arson by black protesters. A case to be made but the damage was done.

Jealously Guarding their Privileges

For as long as white Americans are allowed to enjoy the lion's share of jobs and posts within state institutions, they are able to hold back the tide of progress in favour of racial minorities. And it could also be argued that in the interests of securing election victories either side of the two-term Democratic/Obama administration, Republican representatives have tended to sanction white interests, whether officially or not, in the interests of their constituents.

And all in the interest of securing their overwhelming white privilege in all walks of life.

Concluding Summary

Finally, it remains the case that while white rage can and does extend to other minorities, as mentioned in the beginning of this chapter, the primary target of this rage remains that of black or Afro- Americans.

Chapter 5

Why Racism is a Threat to All of Us

Introduction

No question has been asked at this point. The opening to this chapter is deliberate It professes a statement of fact.

Racism is a threat to all of us.

But as always, it is necessary to substantiate statements or claims made; in this instance, particularly on behalf of those who feel that they are not entirely convinced. Or are blissfully ignorant of the challenges faced by those negatively affected by racism.

There can be no such thing. Ignorance is not bliss.

This chapter attempts to substantiate the very fact that racism is indeed a threat; doing so in the following manner.

The chapter begins by briefly outlining a few examples of racial polarization from a historical perspective. But before that; perhaps it is necessary to understand what is meant by polarization and, more specifically; racial polarization.

Also note that on the global scale, case studies have concluded that racism is a threat. Closer to home – that is to say that the reader is based in North America – an astounding claim has also been made.

That racism is a threat to National Security. So, in this sense, the argument could be made that racism should be regarded with the same seriousness as, say, global terrorism. And perhaps those vested with the powers and duties to act in the interests of national security do so.

To stamp out racism in a diligent and humane manner?

Historical Examples of Racial Polarization

When people are deliberately or voluntarily polarized, they are apart from each other. There are, further, two parallel accounts of forced racial polarization in recent history. And today, polarization across all walks of life and culture have been both voluntary and forced.

In the interests of health, safety and security, people have endeavored to keep their 'social distance' to stave off infection from the COVID-19 virus. It is pertinent to note this because there are those who remember what it is like to be forced apart, prevented from doing what is their basic human right.

Millions of black Americans remember the years of racial segregation during the post-World War Two Years. So too, millions more South Africans during what was known globally as the apartheid years.

Global Case Studies Based on History

But it must always be remembered that it was not only black Americans who were deliberately polarized, both structurally and legislatively. The reaction to the wave of immigration at the turn of the previous century saw to it that millions of Poles, Italians, East Europeans, Europeans of the poorer economic classes, and in particular, Jewish Europeans, were forced to huddle in cramped, squalid conditions and excluded from opportunities across the board.

Indeed, the most horrendous case of racial polarization led to the mass extermination of around six million Jews by the Nazi (National Socialist) regime of Germany before and during the Second World War.

And indeed, previously, going back into the previous century, pogroms far and wide were carried across parts of Europe, Tsarist and Soviet Russia, and even America. Apart from the widespread persecution, death was always the final consequence of racism.

Global Case Studies Based on Current Trends

It is disheartening to note further that Israeli Jews, particularly those who have grim recollections of the previous century's Holocaust, continue to persecute Palestinians of Muslim and Arab descent. Their polarization is visual as well as emotional.

It must be noted that the USA is not unique or isolated in its treatment of racial and/or cultural minorities. Elsewhere in the world, racial (and cultural) oppression and suppression is rife.

In contrast to the way in which the Israeli regime and Israelis treat (Muslim) Palestinians, two current events come to light. In both China and Myanmar, Muslim minorities are being brutally oppressed. While Myanmar Muslims are being denied local opportunities, some managing to flee into neighboring Bangladesh, Chinese Muslims are being held in concentration camps, much akin to those in which European Jews were being held during the brutal Nazi era.

Racism is a National Security Threat

Given that citizens' lives and livelihoods are harmed by ongoing acts of structural racism, as well as the reactions to it, it is hard to imagine that racism at large is not a National Security Threat.

Sherrilyn Ifill, president of the NAACP Legal Defense & Educational Fund, published ground-breaking reports in national news carrier, The Washington Post, on reports released by the Senate Intelligence Committee on alleged Russian interference during the 2016 elections. There were also other studies done by Oxford

University and cybersecurity New Knowledge researchers.

What was revealed?

That the Russian government wished to 'sow discord and confusion' amongst the voting public. There were also alleged attempts to deceive the African-American populace. Furthermore, it is apparent that there is a deliberate attempt by the state to suppress those on the voters' rolls.

It is alleged that foreign powers that be wish to exploit the country's racial divisions further in their own interests.

But the fact remains. Voter apathy continues to be widespread, with or without racial conflict, whereby every four years substantially less than half the country's eligible voters turn up to vote.

US-based (policy) think-tank, the Pacific Council on International Policy, has documented further observations on the perceived or real threats to national security, this time, as a result of institutionalized racism.

The observation was made that the COVID-19 pandemic has merely served to heighten existing racial tensions. The Pacific Council's report that if Americans do not address their race relations, they will weaken their local and international influence.

Furthermore, noting that proportionally more people are incarcerated in the United States than anywhere else in the world. But the majority of the country's prison population are 'people of color'.

The question being asked at this time is why more people of color are being arrested for drug-related offenses while meaningful healthcare is offered to white people instead to treat their drug- related addictions.

Concluding Statement

In conclusion, could it be argued that racism as a national security threat is not being treated with the same amount of seriousness as, say, terrorism would is as a result of the inherent institutional and structural racism not coming close to negatively affecting the country's majority white population?

At the same time, could it be that sectors of the white population perceive racial minorities as a threat to their existence and cultural way of life by the very fact of their actions; physical, verbal and structural.

Chapter 6

Psychology of Racism and its Poisonous Consequences

Introduction

"The function, the very serious function of racism is distraction. It keeps you from doing your work. It keeps you explaining, over and over again, your reason for being."

Toni Morrison

It is worthwhile repeating the opening injunction utilized in the first chapter of this book. It could be relevant to this chapter.

One angle that could also be taken is the imagining of a society devoid of racism. Think of this from an economic point of view and ask yourself; just how much more progress could be made, how much could be done.

How much more could be achieved if there were no loopholes and stigmatizations, whether institutionalized or structural.

This chapter explores the very psychology of racism and the consequences thereof. And by that, read poisonous. And just think what happens to the human body when it is forced to or accidentally ingests poison.

If it doesn't become grievously ill, it could die if not treated accordingly. This, in reality, is what happens when a person is victimized through racism.

An Historical Example

February, 1960.

A Greensboro, NC lunch counter.

Four black American students passively resisted racist legislation by sitting down to lunch in a whites-only cafeteria.

Their seemingly docile resistance subsequently had a tremendous influence for black Americans, as well as their white sympathizers across the country.

But the stress of acting out took its toll on these fine young men. In honor of their actions, today's Ethnic & Health in America Series raises awareness of the psychological consequences of racism and discrimination for the victims.

It is said that the psychological weight did have a negative impact on public health's ability to handle extraordinary caseloads. Add to this the traumatized returnees from the Vietnam War, both white and black.

High Levels of Stress & Anxiety

It is widely known that high levels of stress and anxiety have negative consequences for the human body and mind. But the health of the average African-American family, to say nothing of those trapped in sociologically-driven cycles of poverty is exacerbated as a result of having to deal with racism on a daily basis.

This phenomenon dispels the myth that black Americans are inferiorly (genetically) disposed in terms of their health and wellness in comparison to white Americans who, by and large, lead a far more privileged and prosperous existence.

The Toxicology Report

Studies have revealed that racism is indeed toxic. USC and UCLA scientists have revealed that the experience of racism increases inflammation levels amongst African Americans. As a result, they are more at risk of chronic illness.

An associate professor of psychology and psychiatry at USC remarked that conclusive results showed that victimization as a result of racism does lead to an inflammatory response.

Pope Francis & the Physical Symptoms of Racism

"Rivers do not drink their own water; trees do not eat their own fruit; the sun does not shine on itself and flowers do not spread their fragrance for themselves. Living for others is a rule of nature. We are all born to help each other. No matter how difficult it is. Life is good when you are happy; but much better when others are happy because of you."

Pope Francis

It is also worthwhile including Pope Francis's statement on the essence of human and natural life. Because it is relevant to this section as well.

All living matter survives, or not, as a result of its ability to respond to stressors, infections and injury. As a result, immune systems are required to repair damage caused. Any signs of inflammation in the body is in reaction to countering the threat or repair of damage caused.

But if the body is placed under stress for prolonged periods of time, its ability to deal with chronic inflammation could be significantly weakened. This could lead to heart and neurodegenerative diseases as well as cancer.

Is it any wonder then that, statistically speaking, black Americans are far more prone to such diseases, as well as shortened lifespans, than their white counterparts?

In understudying the reasons for high levels of stress and anxiety, the studies revealed the complexities of dealing with racism. For instance, there is heightened awareness when dealing with poverty and/or financial stress. But there is never complete realization when dealing with any form of discrimination.

It is further argued that while there is always the capacity to deal with everyday challenges, racial discrimination as a chronic stressor cannot be controlled. This argument could even be compared with another complexity of human existence.

Apart from having to deal with the ongoing prejudice, people who identify themselves within the LGBTQ communities are further faced with the reality that they cannot truly alter the way they were born.

How Racism Affects Black American Women

Another prolonged study took a look at the high incidence of breast cancer amongst black American women. It was revealed that encounters with racism as victim did lead to increased incidences of breast cancer.

And a more recent study reveals the effects of racism on those black Americans who suffer from higher than average levels of hypertension. By and large, it is alleged that health care professionals and academics either dismiss or disguise many of the health-related claims laid bare in this chapter.

Furthermore, the argument goes that the study of race-related influences on health and wellbeing remain grossly underfunded.

Conclusion

There is added pressure for those black or African-Americans who find themselves rooted in the country's lowest socio-economic classes, finding themselves classed as needy and/or lazy. That they are disadvantaged further affects their self-worth and dignity or the lack thereof.

Because the realities of racism on black Americans are not being addressed from a health and wellness perspective, valuable members of the community, by and large, are lost due to the occurrences of illness and preventable diseases.

That being said, economic opportunities are also lost.

How Racism Creates Distorted Hierarchies of Human Value

Introduction

This chapter further explores the consequences of racism and its harmful effects on predominantly racial minorities.

The thesis of distorted hierarchies in this chapter utilizes the scientific analogies drawn to both substantiate and counter racism.

This ideal in the sense that the chapter's overriding theme of undermining human value does not need to rely solely on popular concepts and arguments drawn from heightened and academic perspectives influenced by politics, religion, economics and culture.

The academic perspectives drawn on and highlighted in this chapter coincide with other sub-themes such as history, propaganda, theories of evolution, as well as the philosophy of enlightenment racialism to which the reader will be introduced in due course.

Finally, in working against the ingrained realities of distorted hierarchies, this chapter allows the highest body that endeavors to dictate or advocate, as well as govern how societies should live, to have the final say.

Academic & Historical Perspectives

Stanford University historian George Fredrickson produced an academic but abridged account of the history of racism.

The argument goes that examinations of human equality were utilized to promote racism. This book could be examined alongside of the original credo of the US Constitution in which it deems to state that all men are equal before the law and God.

Of course, it is a well-known fact that the Constitution only served the interests of some and excluded or denigrated others (black slaves, Native American tribes).

In essence, racism evolved as the universal powers that be sought to contradict or exploit the original ideals of egalitarianism. This contradiction manifested itself in the exclusionary treatment of specified ethnic groups.

Further, there was an innate rejection of the notion of 'organically hierarchical societies'. And today, those black Americans, particularly those bereft of a decent education, need to appreciate the historical significance of living in the ghetto.

Because while their ancestors were toiling in the cotton fields of wealthy Southerners, European minority migrants, alongside of leading a servile existence, were also subjected to class or racial separation and ghettoized.

Less than Fully Human

Alongside of nineteenth to twentieth century Italian, Irish and Polish migrants living under squalid, cramped conditions in some of the country's largest and most economically active cities, most notably New York, the most notorious physical exemplar of ghettoization occurred on the European continent in the form of (German) Nazi repression of Jews who were inherently classified as sub-human or less than human through the distorted theories of National Socialism.

But the ideals of National Socialism as well as the ideas expounded in Adolf Hitler's Mein Kampf are rooted in history, both cultural and

scientific. For the sake of brevity, this chapter goes back no further than the end of the eighteenth century.

Enlightenment Racialism

And introduces you to a radical concept known as Enlightenment rationalism. When founded, it was to replace notions of faith and superstition. And within thirty years, into the nineteenth century, would sprout Charles Darwin's evolutions of species.

Darwin came to the final conclusion that numerous species were inferior to others. This theory did not exclude the human race.

Science was being used to arrive at concluding the differences between principle and practice. And so it went that science was now being used to validate or justify the discrimination of specified racial groups.

Formulated or convoluted scientific explanations were being used to warn influential sectors of society against inherent biological dangers such as racial interbreeding. Medical scientists and anthropologists went on to claim that mixed or tainted blood would, over time, lead to men and women becoming less fertile and ultimately sterile.

By the early twentieth century, George Mendel's pioneering work would inspire geneticists to claim that marriage between distant races or cultures would ultimately lead to what they termed genetic disharmonies.

Distortions & Propaganda of Biology

Further rationalization of these 'scientific' theories would inspire the development and institutionalization of race-based legislation. Four twentieth century examples are well worth highlighting. Germany's National Socialism policies were harsh in the extreme.

Because not only were Jews subjugated and ultimately annihilated, so too 'Aryan' Germans who were deemed to be physically and mentally inferior. Included in this group of people were the physically and mentally disabled as well as homosexuals.

Policies of eugenics and miscegenation were put in practice in newly independent Australia where native Aboriginal children were abducted from their family centers and placed within white families.

In the aftermath of the Second World War both the United States and South Africa would go on to segregate by law black citizens, known variously as negroes, natives and Bantu, but not yet African- American or African.

Now at this point, the reader may have been correct to assume that this late into the twenty-first century, in an era and spirit of freedom, democracy and equality, such warped theories against racial interbreeding would be laid to rest.

Distorted Laws of Evolution & other Sexual Distortions

But no.

Glayde Whitney is a 'renowned' geneticist and past President of the Behavior Genetics Association.

But he is also a renowned speaker amongst neo-Nazi gatherings.

Earlier, the reader was informed on how racism has had a negative impact on mostly black Americans. But Whitney disagrees.

He believes that health-related complications, as well as high infant death rates, amongst African Americans arose as a result of the effects of what he called hybrid incompatibilities.

And furthermore, it is claimed in the interests of securing the integrity of gene pools, racial prejudice is not only necessary, it is natural.

Needless to say that there have been further propagations attempting to explain why certain race groups are 'less well- endowed' than others. These propagandist theories continue explain (away) why certain race groups are more prone to commit crimes and lack the ability to exercise (sexual) restraint.

Enough of that, readers.

Let's give the last word on hierarchical distortions of human value to the highest body that seeks to influence and, where able to do so, govern how societies across the globe should live.

UN Universal Declaration of Human Rights has the Final Say

After the Second World War finally came to an end, a group of renowned scientists were hosted by the newly formed United Nations, Educational, Scientific and Cultural Organization (UNESCO).

All the scientists gathered issued various statements to counter the notions of racial difference. They not all have agreed, one and the same. But when it came down to the final knock on the gavel, the earliest UNESCO gathering were unanimous in their proclamations.

Basic human rights, to be enjoyed by all, could never be influenced by scientific conclusions on the racial characteristics of human beings.

It was declared that whether the scientific claims were indeed valid or utterly ludicrous, they should not stand in the way of establishing the foundations for creating a universal society in which all, no matter their differences on any level, could enjoy the privileges of human existence and without impeding on those who could be perceived to be in the minority or fragile.

Concluding Statement

And so to speak of theories of evolution, this historic gathering was the first chapter in the evolution of the United Nation's Universal Declaration of Human Rights. George Orwell, British essayist and writer of the renowned dystopian texts 1984 and Animal Farm, would be pleased.

And those who enforced their separate but equal policies on those they sought to subjugate, would be rolling in their graves.

Segregation of America

Introduction

In order to appreciate how the country was historically and politically segregated, it is necessary to begin understanding the very definition of segregation as it was applied.

A useful exercise for this chapter is correlating America's segregationist policies with that of another country that surely needs little introduction. And in both countries, the literary use of the sign should be worthy of observation.

Also note that, still to this day, segregation amongst these countries' peoples are not entirely governed by law but in private practice as well. Go further back in twentieth century history and you will also see how perceived libertarian statesmen were also prone to favour segregation or racism.

Segregation – A Definition

But as always, there is a silver lining.

In the pursuit of eradicating all forms of racism, it is worthwhile recounting how segregationist policies of the past were countered.

But how to interpret segregation?

At least the Oxford English Dictionary is clear about this.

According to the dictionary definition; to segregate means to set apart or come apart from the rest. Furthermore, to segregate or separate basically means to isolate.

And so it goes that the definition becomes more acute when segregation implies the separation of racial or cultural communities, whether enforced, deliberate or voluntary.

The Use of Signs

One of the most effective yet passive means of segregating American citizens based on the color of their skin was to use signage in all walks of public life.

In the early days of legislated segregation, signs would specifically depict where Coloreds were allowed to drink from a public fountain or walk along designated sidewalks.

The use of such signage, however effective it was, was quite ludicrous. Picture this scenario. In the analogy of one public drinking fountain both white and black Americans would be using said fountain.

But signposting would depict from which angle or side white people or people of color could drink their water. And while racial prejudice was rife amongst many white Americans, it would not be unusual to see rare incidents of people of opposing races sharing the same public facilities at the same time.

Comparing US Segregation with Apartheid South Africa

But the use of signs was far more brutally enforced in South Africa. Every opportunity was taken to diminish black South Africans' status as human beings.

For instance, a bus stop would quite clearly state that it was reserved for 'whites only'. Black commuters would simply have to take the hint and move on. But to speak of busses and other modes of public transportation.

While dozens of black South Africans were brutally suppressed during the infamous Sharpeville protest, one decent, little old lady sparked a countrywide mass boycott of public transportation in protest of racial segregation laws. Furthermore, black South Africans were further subjected to routine checks by South Africa's equivalent of law enforcement officers.

Hyper segregation

And any transgression of segregationist laws would usually lead to fines or incarceration.

Now, the practice of what is known as hyper segregation is actually nothing new but the term will be for a majority of readers at this point in time.

Let this section briefly introduce you to the concept.

As late as the nineteen-eighties, no less than twenty segregation measures were catalogued. This catalogue was further reduced to five dimensions of residential segregation. The study revealed that black Americans were deemed to be racially segregated as a result of these five dimensions.

These dimensions continued to be applied to a majority of inner cities across the country. They were defined as – centralization, clustering, concentration, evenness and exposure.

Financial Segregation

Strictly speaking, financial segregation was not, is not legislated.

But it was structural. To use the example of Federal Housing Administration practices, a blind eye view was taken when qualifying black American families were denied housing loans for spurious reasons such as their sought-after neighborhoods being 'in decline'.

Furthermore, such areas in decline had to make way for the building of elevated highways. In the process thousands of black-owned homes were destroyed.

Where were affected families to go then? Well, they were summarily relocated to what is, still to this day, widely known as 'the projects'.

Such brutality could easily be compared to the relocation of millions of Black, Colored and Indian South Africans after South Africa's Nationalist government promulgated the Group Areas Act.

Racism by the President

Basically, people of color were forcibly removed from respectable neighborhoods, their places taken by whites, and relocated far outside of urban centers to move into what came to be known as 'matchbox' houses.

US President, Woodrow Wilson, is widely heralded as the libertarian but hapless founding father of the League of Nations.

He paved the way for the establishment of this world governing body during the closing stanzas of the First World War into which this president reluctantly led his country.

Hailed as a libertarian the world over, Wilson appears to have had no qualms about oppressing his own people.

Another Comparison with South Africa

It is recorded that President Wilson did not oppose segregationist policies carried out by heads of federal civil service agencies. He never opposed the country earliest segregation laws. Another public figure held in high esteem was South African Prime Minister Jan Smuts.

He is widely regarded as one of Winston Churchill's closest allies during the global fight against Hitler and Nazi Germany. And yet, Smuts was a staunch believer in the separation of the races and that non-white South Africans were inherently inferior to their white counterparts, destined to a life of menial labor.

Nevertheless, Smut's philosophic presentations to the newly- founded United Nations were summarily dismissed.

Historic Challenges to Segregation in America

And while Britain's WWII hero was humiliated at the polls, Smuts went on to lose against a more brutal oppressor in the form of the National Party during that country's 1948 whites-only general election.

Now, those readers who remain inherently opposed to any form of racism can only draw inspiration from the historic accounts of opposition to segregation in America. Arguably, the most famous example of public outrage occurred in Montgomery, Alabama.

To this day, it seems hard to believe that it was that little old lady, one Mrs Rosa Parks, who sparked a mass wave of passive resistance and inherently peaceful protest against racial segregation.

The Anti-miscegenation Laws

All because she refused to move to the back of the bus to make way for a white passenger.

But let it not be forgotten that protest action was not always peaceful, since the turn of the twentieth century right to the present day.

After all, it was Malcolm X who declared that US-based racism should be defeated 'by any means necessary'.

One of the most horrendous segregation laws was surely that of preventing people from loving each other in the form of anti- miscegenation laws. These laws essentially prevented men and women from marrying across color lines.

But while South Africa's Population Registration Act was enjoying its infancy during the nineteen century, the US's miscegenation laws were surreptitiously and laboriously repealed during the brief tenure of John F Kennedy who asked the people what they could do for their country.

Concluding Statement

And not what their country can do for them. And yet.

Perhaps there is some truth in what Mr Kennedy said.

While racial segregation laws were widely scrapped by the late sixties, a new wave of civic protest action, alongside that of anti-war demonstrations, in the form of the Stonewall incident.

And so it goes today that lesbian, gay and transgendered men and women are now legally permitted to marry in the interests of love, as is also the case in democratic South Africa. And years later, the USA's first black American President would include a transgendered woman in his cabinet.

What comes from acting on behalf of others.

Chapter 7

How to Deal with Racism

Introduction

After the previous chapter closed on a historical and inspirational high, perhaps those who remain inherently opposed to racism and particularly those who are victimised by it should find working through this chapter pleasant rather than laborious.

That's because this chapter is practically-inclined.

The reader is going to be provided with brief demonstrations and/or lessons on how to deal with racism in familiar walks of life, from the workplace to social media circles.

It begins with a ten-point plan. And indeed, it does offer suggestions on how to deal with racism in the workplace. But there is a warning. This has something to do with the fallible habit of doing nothing as opposed to taking action.

A ten-point Plan

It should be pleasing to note that perhaps a majority of readers of minority status who, in turn, are enjoying a higher socio-economic status than their forefathers are not subjected to racism as was the case in the past.

And yet it remains rife.

And when racism does hit you in unexpected ways, you may find yourself at a loss. What to do when your person is subjected to racism in any form? Here is a ten-point plan that you could study.

1. Always keep calm.

2. Act with kindness.

3. Be prepared to call your local law enforcement agency if you are physically threatened.

4. Do not act against the offender but rather against the action.

5. Document the incident.

6. But do not record personal details.

7.   Do not act emotively.

8.   But remain prepared to expose the racist act.

9.   At this stage, it may be pointless endeavouring to educated the offending other.

10. Finally, there is always this. Simply do nothing. But is this a good thing in the interest of ensuring that such an act is not repeated?

This question is examined in the following section.

Dangers of Non-responsiveness

The contentious issue of non-responsiveness takes its cue from the workplace, a productive environment where the minority reader may be spending most of his or her time in any given day.

It is advised that, specifically for those who will probably not be affected by racism, that both inaction and ignorance are probably two of the worst counters to racism.

It is further advised that not even subtle and yet derogatory remarks, even those that are intended as humorous, should not be ignored either. The harsh reality of actual racism is that it is no longer acceptable to dismiss allegations of racism.

Dealing with Social Media Racism

They do need to be interrogated in an appropriate manner.

Today, one of the worst and most regular manifestations of racism is that which takes place within social media circles. In essence, such

acts of racism are cowardly because the offended person is at a viral distance and in no position to react physically.

And yet, you are always in a position to act. Here, you do so in writing but bear in mind that your reaction will be recorded. So it remains essential to react in a calm and polite manner without resorting to undesirable language.

And even if you feel disempowered to react, you can still act. It is not quite the same as doing nothing. There are bodies that govern the ethics of social media activities.

When to call Law Enforcement

If not a non-governmental or consumer watchdog agency, you can still report the online incident to your local law enforcement agency. And you will be in a position to level a charge of crimen injuria against the offender.

Through diligence, it is quite possible to locate said offender who may have thought it was possible to remain obscure, even anonymous online. But conventional reporting to law enforcement will always entail responding to public acts that are irredeemably a physical threat in the even that no act of public violence has been carried out.

Responding to Racism in the Media

The media environment is as broad-based as they come.

It is even in your kitchen in the form of the advertising on your everyday household items or condiments.

Those who blithely wish to dismiss this form of (extreme) civic action may be welcome to do so, you may feel otherwise. Even so, even if you detected a hint of racism on the side of your pickle jar, you could still report it.

There are advertising boards of control to which you can report. The same goes for your social media platforms, your daily newsprint and even your favorite pay per view channels. And these days, most functioning democracies have their own version of a Human Rights Commission to which you could report suspected racist behaviour in the media.

There are also non-governmental bodies which actively campaign against racism and similar acts of hate and discrimination to which you could report.

Racism in the Workplace

For instance, if you are acutely gender sensitive or (unconventionally) gender orientated, you can report directly to a relevant NGO agency, as could be the case when a transgendered woman is denied equal opportunities within the work environment and subsequently reports this abuse to her local LGBTQ+ support group.

Fortunately for most American citizens who form part of minority groups, legislation does protect them against racial, gender and sexual discrimination. But it remains the case on just how far public representatives are prepared to go in the protected interests of minorities.

How to Deal with Racism in the Workplace

But stakeholders across the board, whether they be company owners or staff supervisors, are empowered to act without having to resort to third party intervention, whether public, private or part of a rights advocacy groups.

There are practical but salient steps that can be followed. This chapter closes with practical steps that could be followed to deal with reported real or suspected racism within the workplace.

Even if you are not in a position of authority, you could show leadership potential. While you're not on an out and out brag-fest, you could be impressing some of your superiors, your colleagues, and perhaps even future employers with this exemplary behaviour.

But of course, these steps only become necessary when there is clear evidence or suspicion of racism on your shop or office floor, even amongst customers.

1. Communicate & educate

In this discussion, you need to be frank but always respectful. You need to be able to ask questions, asking perhaps what was intended by the racist remark made.

Should there be a passive reaction, you could endeavour to educate the offender. More often than not, fortunately, people act out in a racist manner more from ignorance than malicious intent.

2. Communicating with others

There may be the possibility that the guilty offender has acted out against fellow-employees. Particularly in the event that no one has spoken up (more often than not, they are afraid to do so) you need to ask if this is so.

But you will need to do so with discretion and initially only with those you trust implicitly.

3. Promote your self-worth

If you are in the racial minority and have been harmed or offended by racism in the workplace, one of the best and most decent things you can do is set a professional example.

You need to show the guilty offender that you are here to work, and that you are doing the job you've been task with because you are valued for your skills and knowledge.

Unless you are up for promotion, it is not for others to determine your value in the workplace. That is for you to do.

Furthermore, rivalling co-workers could be guilty of racism if they perceive you to be a threat to their status.

Often that is never the case and it is usual that such co-workers need to examine their own shortcomings.

4.   Seek representation

Assume then that all avenues – as suggested above – have been exhausted and come to naught, it is imperative that you seek legal representation. If the organization is a large and professional one, its human resources department should be able to assist you in this matter.

But because this department essentially represents the interests of the company, there may be reluctance to do so. Nevertheless, you should be able to approach your region's governmental labor department for assistance in such matters.

Concluding Statement

After reading through this chapter, are you not feeling more comfortable? Always just remember that you are never alone in this. There are others who may be similarly afflicted. And if needs be, never give up on seeking out third party assistance.

It might still be hard for some of you to accept but truly, not everyone is racist or retains supremacist tendencies.

Chapter 8

How to Deal with the Toxic Mind-sets & Change Them

Introduction

If you, yourself have what is known as a toxic mind-set then you'll need to do some navel gazing before you cast aspersions on others with whom you have the tendency to disagree.

But whether you are Black, White, Native, Hispanic, Purple or Pink, many of you may not even be aware that you have what is known as the toxic-mind set. This could be challenging in the sense that should you be faced with racism, and feel victimized in the process, how are you going to react?

It may not always happen. But still; it could. You could overreact.

Your Toxicology Report

And that could be dangerous.

In more ways than one. It could be dangerous not only to you as a person, but to your livelihood, and perhaps more especially; to your loving family.

It is not always easy. Putting yourself first does allow you to at least be positive and make progressive inroads in your life. But it may become challenging when you are required to put the needs of your family first.

Many young men and women, black or white, often put their lives on hold just so that their parents can be happy. But what if they are wrong?

Understanding the Terminologies

Sad to say it; but some folks can be, and are; racist.

Apart from re-educating yourself, you need to educate them as well.

But before you get to that point in your life, try and understand and appreciate the terms raised in this chapter.

What does it mean to be toxic? And what, really, does the (human) mind-set entail?

In basic terms, when something is toxic, it is poisonous. An earlier chapter highlighted the danger of being poisoned. Fortunately, there is always treatment and cure. So if the mind-set has a tendency to be toxic, it does need to be treated, and cured, before it reaches its point of no return

When addressing the racist mind-set amongst your elders, adopt the positive mind-set and utilize this old adage;

You are never too old to change.

But how does one define the human mind-set in the context of this entire book that seeks to address both racism and, never mind white, but; human fragility.

What do you understand by the Mind-set?

And what do you think of this. Don't you think the time is rife to adjust the iconic hashtag that is Black Lives Matter to - All Lives Matter?

Look for leadership on this matter and perhaps look no further than Martin Luther King and Nelson Mandela. Try and read up on what they had to say on, let's just say it for now, this matter; the toxic mind-set and how to address it.

The mind-set that you adopt is basically your way of thinking, perceiving and believing. But it could also be influenced by what you have been taught by your parents, for better or for worse, and by what you have been indoctrinated with in your community or country, whether you're in the racial minority.

It is All About having the Right Attitude

Or majority.

Having the right attitude about important issues such as racism is essential. But first this. What do you understand and appreciate about being indoctrinated as opposed to being influenced?

When you are influenced – for better or for worse – you are sometimes inspired by what others say or do. Like Nelson Mandela and Martin Luther King. And even Malcolm X. What they did, and what they sacrificed so that you can all, one day, be free.

And true freedom does not necessarily entail that you are free from racist legislation and structural racism. It means that you are free in your own mind (and heart) to lead by example.

Negative Mind-set Flaws

For instance, you achieve nothing by reacting antagonistically to racist insults and actions. Read the previous chapter on how to deal with racism.

To be indoctrinated could lead to a toxic mind-set. The indoctrination doesn't have to come from the racist/racial antagonists alone. It could also come from those whom you sometimes look up to for inspiration and leadership.

Indoctrination could lead you on the path to radicalism. In history, and just think about this for a second, in history, in terms of the end-game that led to the scrapping of all forms of racist legislation during the nineteen-sixties, which form of resistance turned out to be more effective.

The Positive Mind-set

That of Malcolm X's, and for that matter, the Black Panther Movement's actions that resorted to violent retaliations that led to lives being lost?

Or that of the massive wave of passive resistance led by Nobel Peace Prize recipient, Martin Luther King? King, as well as Mandela (and before him, Albert Luthuli (also a Peace Prize recipient), were inspired by Indian behemoth, Mahatma Ghandi's passive resistance that ultimately led to India's Independence from Great Britain.

It is up to you to decide which form of resistance remains more effective. But one thing that could be said is that these historic events would not have been possible without the positive mind-set.

Dealing with Change

Everyone, at some stage of their lives, is faced with having to make important changes.

And if you have encountered this in your own lives, you'll know that change has never been easy. But to adopt the positive mind-set once more, always try to think of change in these terms.

Change is just as good as taking a vacation.

Nevertheless, it remains challenging for the white majority to adjust to change whereby more minority groups are empowered to embrace new opportunities that were always the preserve of the white population.

How to deal with this if you are in the minority?

As hard as it may seem, it may be necessary for you to be as understanding as possible.

Change you can Believe In

So, while change does happen, it invariably does not happen overnight.

Take Barack Obama's history-making campaign for example. Many of the policies that he campaigned for are only now filtering through.

And try as he may, it has not been possible for Obama's successor, Donald Trump, to overturn the reforms sought and achieved during the Obama administration years.

And what was it that Obama said during his campaign? Here's change that you can believe in. But he also said this much. Change becomes that much easier when you, and others, are prepared to and able to embrace it.

And while many of you have been able to do just that, it remains challenging for the white majority, by and large.

And...Yes You Can!

Even so, positive change (in anyone's life) requires patience and endurance.

You may not be able to overhaul racial and sexual discrimination in the workplace overnight. But if you are in it for the long haul, said discrimination will ultimately be rescinded. Again, do read what was said in the closing stanzas of the previous chapter.

And as far as moms and pops go, well now, that is quite the challenge. But feel and be empowered by this challenge because current legislation is on your side. And if at times the wheels of change appear laggard, there is always your support groups.

Leading by the Obama Example

That's another lesson for you to take home with you in endeavoring

to deal with and reverse toxic mind-sets.

Do not ever expect to campaign alone. Apart from the fact that there are plenty of others who may feel the same way as you do, there are also those who have the ability to effect change, wherever necessary and not necessarily by any means necessary.

Barack Obama had the good fortitude of a supportive administration. It is no accident that he chose Joe Biden, then something of an elder statesman, to be his wise counsellor. He even had Senator Hillary Clinton, as well as others, to lean on.

Conclusion

Obama never acted alone. While he is well-known to have his own (personal) views on, say, affirmative action, he would always consult, engage and listen before reaching for his executive pen to sign race-based reforms into law.

Dealing with the toxic mind-set does require resilience. But real change, so often, comes from within.

Chapter 9

How to Reorient Conversations About Racism

Introduction

If there is one thing that you and your fellow readers can agree to, it is this.

Racism is real. It exists. As for those who disagree, therein lies the challenge for you. If no conversation exists about racism, then perhaps it is time for you to reignite the flame.

But generally speaking, that conversation is ongoing. Unfortunately, it is not always pleasant. While disagreement on an approach to take towards a racist encounter could be healthy, such discord could end up being toxic.

The social media forum is a perfect example. It is ironic in the sense that it is generally a free and open forum where everyone is able to have his or her say.

Who gets to Start The Conversation?

But it remains possible for far-right groups to infiltrate the discussion.

This is, however, where you get to reorient the conversation you're having. It is a case of having to resort to harsh action. If, for instance, you are hosting the forum, it remains within your rights and ability to exclude those who bring no value to the conversation, particularly if they resort to the extremes of resorting to racist remarks.

When starting the conversation, you still need to implicitly state your targeted objectives.

You also need to lay the ground rules in terms of the expected behavioural patterns. And before you welcome anyone into your social circle, you do need to be prepared to screen them.

What Characterizes a Proper Conversation?

The social media discussion, by way of example, applies to all settings. Your town meeting. Schools, churches and even sports clubs. And certainly, the workplace discussion too.

While it is sensible to impose stringent ground rules under challenging conditions, you still need to leave the window open for opposing views. How else to better understand what the other is thinking, and what he inherently believes, whether under influence or indoctrination?

Even so, there is always room for decorum. Particularly if you are engaging with opposing views, you are required to remain polite. As hard as it may seem to some, endeavour always to raise your views objectively.

The Art of being a Good Listener

And leave your emotions at home.

Becoming a good listener requires practice for the garrulous speaker.

You are always entitled to have your say. But endeavour to think carefully about what you want to say and then keep your remarks brief and to the point.

This too, takes practice.

Thereafter, sit back and listen. That's all you need to do. Listen carefully to what that person has to say. Along the way you should be able to make important points which you can encapsulate in your responding remarks.

Of course, the only time you may be required to intervene is when the addressee resorts to racist or derogatory remarks.

Conversation vs Consultation

If you are a good listener, then you will know when to intervene.

A proper conversation is also knowledge-based. Yes, you are allowed to speak from experience, particularly if it is in context with the conversation. But at some stage, the conversation does need to end.

So, what happens next? And indeed, what could be happening before the conversation even begins. There is always the consultation process. You are able to set the agenda of your discussion in this manner.

And after the conversation, you are able to interview those attendees who made valuable or qualified contributions. Because now you are using the consultation process to formulate policy.

How things get done in the White House. Or not.

First Engage then Reorient

This section can be carved further into two sub-sections. Firstly, what does it mean to engage. Thereafter, how to reorient the conversation. Also know when reorientation is required.

Structural Engagement

Racism is structural. That much was laid bare in previous chapters. But so too the response to it, and it is not necessarily toxic. But what does it take to engage structurally. In order to create a sense of cohesion going forward, do make certain that those you engage with are qualified to provide input which could be invaluable in formulating policy.

What does Reorientation entail?

Here, a sense of redirection is required. This is required when the discussion goes completely off topic. You are able to reorient the conversation if you have been listening carefully, also making recordings of remarks made and reviewing and evaluating them.

About Racism – A Recap

In the context of this chapter, the definition of racism takes a different angle.

To say that someone is racist owing to the (racist, derogatory) remarks he may have made is far too easy. In an open public meeting, observing body language and the tone of voice could leave hints that someone is inherently racist.

He has what are known as supremacist tendencies. In the company of minorities, he is cock-sure of himself. Or is he?

Trying to prove that someone is racist in a social media setting becomes a little more challenging. Because how are you to make such observations, particularly when the addressee is not prone to resorting to emotive (written) language that is inherently racist and/or derogatory.

And furthermore, while no one may explicitly state that he or she is white, for instance, you are sometimes able to make a cultural observation by dint of that person's name.

This remains challenging in the sense that you are required to or prompted to make racial observations which in turn could turn out to be racist.

So, here's another challenge then. Are you able to enter a debate in a dispassionate manner, almost as though no racism existed?

Even if there is no Racism in your Community; do you still Talk About it?

You would have to be living in Utopia for that to exist.

A world utterly devoid of racism. But still. It could happen. While it is isolated in this day and age, there are towns and regions in which there are no manifestations of racism.

And yet still. This how it happens. Policies to do with influx control are above average harsh. Which means to say that racial and cultural minorities seeking greener pastures are luckless in gaining entry to that Promised Land.

So, no racism then? No, not quite that. If you share such sentiments under similar socio-economic circumstances, perhaps now is the time to start this important conversation. Talk about racism at your next town hall meeting.

Dangers of Staying Silent – A Recap

It was former US President Richard Nixon who coined the phrase; the silent majority. And in recent times, right in the middle of the Black Lives Matter Campaign, President Donald Trump has helped himself to this expression to stand by the majority in democratic order.

It is the duty of the sitting president to democratically represent the interests of the majority, even if they are mostly silent, simply getting on with their lives as hard-working Americans generally do. Not so? Not so. Because while the silent majority are helping themselves to their country's riches, numerous minorities are suffering at the hands of prejudice and worse

Concluding Statement

Because they bear the brunt of racial, sexual, gender and cultural abuse, they have no alternative but to speak out, sometimes acting out as well. So, if you classify yourself as being part of the silent majority, do you stay silent indefinitely? Yes, if you harbour racist tendencies. But no if you believe that you could be non-racial or even anti-racist.

Chapter 10

Combatting Racism

Introduction

Nation of Islam convert, Malcolm X combatted racism. Today, Louis Farrakhan still is. So then, if you consider yourself a devout Muslim, do you combat racism in the way that they did, still do.

To continue the comparative thread, left-wing politician Julius Malema has branded South Africa's iconic statesman, as a sell-out (to the white minority). He could argue that Mandela did not combat racism in that country.

And yet, the Nobel Peace Prize winner did. It is recorded in the history books and numerous biographical texts, authorized and unauthorized, that Nelson Mandela combatted racism. But some may argue too that fellow-Nobel Peace Prize recipient, Dr Martin Luther King Jnr did not.

A Two-part Series

He did not combat racism.

It is argued that King Jnr was far too passive. But his peaceful actions, surely, did lead to the eventual emancipation of millions of black Americans. Because in the same decade that he was assassinated, all forms of racist legislation were scrapped

Black Americans were now free to go to the same diners as their fellow white Americans. And seat themselves where they wished to. They could also send their children to decent schools, the very same schools that the silent (mostly white) majority were sending their children to all along.

But still. Far-left radicals may well have a point.

Time to Adopt the Combative Mode?

Before this discussion goes any further, do note that is going to continue into the following chapter – on becoming an anti-racist. It is part and parcel of what it takes to become an anti-racist.

Nevertheless, advocates of combative alternatives to fighting racism, may well have a point. Because fifty years down the line, the evidence is quite clear. While legislative racism may have been scrapped, structural racism continues unabated. US President Barack Obama may well have been combative in dealing with his predecessor's proclaimed axis of evil.

But while he took great strides in legislating for racial and socio- economic reforms, the question has been asked. Was Mr Obama combative in dealing with what was in an earlier chapter referred to as a National Security threat

What essentially is Combat?

Indeed, it was he who confessed to being a greater admirer of the work that Malcolm X did, over that done by the reverend Martin Luther King. But perhaps the president's position needs to be more acutely understood. It is the duty of the president to protect all lives, including white lives. So, how is it possible for him to adopt a combative stance?

In essence, in its literal form, combat entails coming to blows with opposing forces. But figuratively speaking, that is never intended.

Adopting a combative mode does not mean that you need resort to violence.

Think about this for a moment.

Would Dialogue not be Better?

Along the side-lines of physically combatting a racist law enforcement battalion, shops are being looted and burned. And these shops, incidentally, are not always white owned. They are run by minority groups as well, they are being run by your very own brothers and sisters.

It does not seem practical to take this course of action at this point in time. Would expressive dialogue devoid of racist and derogatory remarks not be feasible? This is still a contentious question because it is sometimes argued that derogatory language is a permissible form of retaliation in order to drive home a point.

Time to be Inspired

Does this not call for the proverbial point of order perhaps?

Let's utilize some inspiration to seek out alternative and more practical ways of combatting racism. Let's look at the historical examples set by others. Note that this is in no way a subjective or opinionated line of suggestion. In the spirit of freedom of expression, it does leave the ball in the reader's court.

In lieu of his or her own personal or communal circumstances, the reader should still be able to decide which course of action to take. But at this point in time, it should be argued that the course of action you take should remain legal and constitutional so that it in no way harms others physically or infringes on their rights.

Mahatma Ghandi

The great Ghandi abhorred all forms of physical combat, most of it violent. He not only opposed the racial/racist violence meted out by the British Empire's military and law enforcement agencies, he opposed the great country's internal cultural and religious violence as well, between most the majority Hindus and the minority Muslims.

He opposed it so much that at one point, he went on a fast, in protest against the violence. He fasted for days, almost to the point of dying.

It finally touched the nation's people. They postponed their brutal actions to give peace a chance. But unfortunately, there was to be a return to violence that ultimately split the nation into two states; India (for the Hindus) and Pakistan (for the Muslims).

Nelson Mandela

Nelson Mandela, history records, reluctantly entered into what was known as the armed struggle against the apartheid regime. Becoming the ANC's first commander in chief of its military wing, he was forced to ditch his previous campaign of passive (non-violent) resistance.

But Umkhonto we Sizwe's strategy was to act as saboteurs against the state only and not harm civilian lives, neither black nor white. That innocent lives were ultimately lost could be correlated to what the current US regime often refers to as collateral damage.

But in later years, it was apartheid State President, FW de Klerk, who took the political gamble of releasing Mandela and his comrades from incarceration 'unconditionally'.

Dr Martin Luther King Jnr

This gamble appeared to pay off because within years South Africa finally became a democratic union with Mandela as its first statesman.

Dr Martin Luther King Jnr, however, never got to see his ultimate dream realised. But up to the time that he was assassinated, he remained steadfast in following the passive resistance and non- combative example set by India's Gandhi.

It could be argued that this level of resilience ultimately paid off once the US Government and its Supreme Court finally ruled in favour of scrapping all forms of racist legislation in that country.

But had King Jnr lived, he may have been the first to acknowledge that this outcome was not through his resistance alone.

Malcom X

There were others, mostly notably Nation of Islam convert, Malcolm X who issued the famous mantra;

'By any means necessary'.

And yes, he did advocate the violent alternative of combatting racism. But it has to be argued that, like Mandela advocated, this would only happen once all other forms of (combative and non- combative) dialogue and (physical) protest action were exhausted and did not ultimately yield the desired results.

It is worthwhile mentioning yet another Nation of Islam convert for the purposes of inspiring you to adopt the combative mode, if needs be. Boxing legend, Muhamad Ali, was prepared to sacrifice his World Heavyweight titles and boxing career in order to remain steadfast in his commitment to combating racism.

Understanding what your Leaders had in Mind

As a form of protest against the racist regime, he was prepared to abscond on his conscription into the US Army, even if it meant being imprisoned. He was black. But the nation's folk hero, one Elvis Presley, readily joined the army, portraying himself as a patriot.

But unlike thousands of young black and white Americans, he saw no combat in Vietnam, or elsewhere. You can already see the force of Ali's commitment.

And you can now appreciate what your past leaders had in mind. You should now also appreciate what your current leadership structures have in mind in combatting racism in your communities.

To Be Continued...

But you need to fully understand the agenda set. In order for any form of combative protest to have any sense of credibility, there must be a set preamble with on final objective in mind. It simply cannot be a spontaneous movement, whether linking arms in protest or taking up arms.

Because there is the danger of anarchy.

Combatting racism however it is done, does have its merits. But in order for it to enjoy successful outcomes and be credible as well as acceptable, it needs to be weighted in favour of acting within the ambit of the country's Constitutional laws.

In the next chapter, you should see yourself moving closer towards becoming a full-fledged anti-racist as opposed to being non-racial.

Chapter 11

Beyond the Awareness of Racism & Becoming an Anti-Racist

Introduction

You are already aware of racism.

Unless you are utterly ignorant, you cannot deny that racism does not exist.

But having said that, you may wish to move beyond mere awareness and start playing an active role in combatting racism in your community.

One way of doing that could be by becoming an anti-racist as opposed to merely being non-racist. The differences between these two concepts will be examined in the following chapter that helps pave the way towards teaching your children about racism.

By way of inspiration and example, this chapter continues to prepare you for these exercises; how to become an anti-racist and teaching your children about this social ill.

I Have Fought Against White Domination

It also continues with the comparative thread by referring to anti-racism legends from both America and South Africa, beginning here with the African country.

There can be no denying that, at least in the modern era, no greater advocate of the non-racist and anti-racist stance exists than in the

form of Nelson Mandela. He made one very important proclamation when in the dock on charges of treason against the apartheid state.

He remarked that it was all very well to be fighting against white domination but warned his audience that it would become necessary to fight against black domination as well.

Never, never, And Never Again

Those words were to become prophetic as is now evidenced in South Africa's current political and socio-economic climate whereby racially-inspired policies have been legislated in favour of that country's (black) majority and leaving its (white) minority, by and large, excluded.

He made the point of reminding his fellow-countrymen of the need to move away from all forms of racial discrimination during his inaugural speech. That never again would one racial group impose its will on another.

Equality before the country's law would be the preferred route, and it was concretised when its Constitution, perhaps the most liberal of its kind in the modern era, was signed into law several years later.

The Dream

There is evidence that the country's Constitution is working because, as in America, citizens from all walks of life have been able to approach its Constitution Court to challenge transgressions, particularly of these have been discriminatory.

An old adage suggests that in order for dreams to become a reality, it would have to be supported by action. The old saying goes too that actions speak louder than words. But just what form will this action take?

Will it be passively objectivised through non-racialism? Or will it be actively engaged by becoming an anti-racist? Again, this book does not seek to force its will on the reader.

By Any Means Necessary

It will continue to encourage its readers to make up their own minds on what needs to be done. This same attitude could also be instilled in the readers' children. As children grow older, they should be left to exercise free will but until they reach an age of consent, always under the guardianship of their parents.

Malcolm X and his followers were essentially anti-racists. Because they believed that the passive and legislative alternatives had been futile and a more aggressive approach was subsequently required. A similar stance could still be taken today.

But be reminded always that, as is the case for civic organizations in South Africa, there are legal means of practicing your brand of anti- racism.

Leadership Inspiration – A Recap

You have legal, Constitutional and legislative tools that your former leaders did not always have. The current Black Lives Matter campaign could be seen as clear evidence of acting legally and Constitutionally, whether in public or via social media.

And those of you who have transgressed those boundaries may have felt the brunt of the law. Think about it. Leaders of the past endured long or intermittent periods of incarceration for their actions. But today, you have to ask yourself whether such sacrifices are practical.

The course of action you take today will, of course, have to depend on your community's unique circumstances and the level of racism,

whether structural or extreme, that it has had to endure.

What Malcolm X & Mandela were faced with

Another observation of history needs to be taken into account. Earlier, it was remarked that Mandela led an armed struggle reluctantly. Personally, he may not have favored this combative approach but was required to act democratically and respect the majority view of his movement.

And as a Nation of Islam disciple, it could be argued that Malcolm X was required to observe its documented call to action. It may well surprise many readers that the combative stance that Malcolm X took was moderate in comparison to that movement's leaders.

One further argument could be made in favour of these two struggle icons' actions.

Understanding What Malcolm X Meant

It has to be remembered that they and their constituents literally had their backs to the wall. The combative and anti-racist stance they chose to take could be regarded as both retaliatory and reactionary.

Did they exhaust all legal means in their opposition to racism? By and large, history records that they did. And in history, there are those that took the Nation of Islam hero's words far too literally. Because when he proposed that mainly black Americans oppose racism 'by any means necessary' he did not, strictly speaking, advocate the use of violence.

But he did will men and women to act in self-defense, particularly when law enforcement agencies either failed to come to their aid or acted out as their antagonists.

Adopting the Combative Mode

Be reminded always that in adopting a combative mode does not require you to become physically and/or verbally violent. There are still legal, civic and Constitutional means at your disposal. And before you take to the streets, print media and the airwaves, you do need to listen to what your community have to say, particularly if you have been directly or indirectly elected to represent them.

Nevertheless, there have been cases in recent history in which an individual sparked a process of mass outrage, quite literally, as it turns out. Here is an example beyond the borders of your country.

So; When Does Combat Become Necessary?

It became known as the Arab Spring after a single martyr inspired millions of Muslims across the entire Islamic belt to take to the streets. But this historic example of mass-combative behaviour also provides clear evidence that it does not always succeed.

Certainly, the setting and context is entirely different from yours. These people were prompted to take the 'by any means necessary' stance owing to their lack of legal recourse, and quite tragically, they have been left worse off. If they are not restrained through a more brutal militaristic regime, their country or region has been engulfed in civil war.

Becoming An Anti-Racist

Both Gaddafi Libya and Al-Assad's Syria are examples of the latter, while Egypt remains a case in point in the former case. Armed conflict also becomes possible when third-party sources step forward to assist the oppressed, however ulterior its motives may prove to be.

But surely you will not be challenged with such extremes in becoming an anti-racist. What you do need to prepare yourself for is visibility. Your movements, physically and vocal, will be closely monitored by both those who actively support you and those who perceptively and structurally oppress you and your representative communities.

Engaging actively will always have its challenges.

This Discussion Continues

Learning to overcome them may require you to develop what is known as a thick skin whereby you are always expected to have the courage of your convictions. You can no longer be expected to stand by the side lines or sit on the fence if you will.

Having made your voice thick in your opposition to racism, people, whether they agree or support you, or disagree and actively oppose you, may be expecting more from you. Battle lines may be drawn but it does not necessarily advocate resorting to physical and verbal violence.

And by verbal violence read returning racial or racist remarks with outbursts of your own.

In the next chapter, learn what it takes to be an anti-racist while teaching your children about racism.

Chapter 12

How to Teach Your Children About Racism

Introduction

This chapter attempts to define not just the significance of what it means to be an anti-racist but what it will take to become one.

There is also a need to define in the most simplified or basic terms what may be required of you to live and practice as an anti-racist. Further, as you grow as an anti-racist, you'll be teaching your children about racism.

In order to appreciate the fundamentals of anti-racism, it is necessary to do a comparison with the concept of non-racism.

Further than that, there are other fundamental lessons and concerns that should be tied in with the principles and practices of teaching young children about racism.

What is An Anti-racist?

If you study your dictionary definitions closely enough, you soon learn that being an anti-racist means that you have to take a thoroughly principled and almost uncompromising stance against racism in its entirety.

You could even compare this to the more widely utilised definition of being an anti-Semite. In this case, if you were an anti-Semite, you would have a staunch prejudice of Jews. Of course, should you be anti-racist, you could hardly be against Jews.

Because to be an anti-racist means that you should be against all forms of prejudice levelled against all mostly minority race groups, cultures and religions.

Differences between Anti-racism & Non-racism

As a practicing anti-racist, you are literally taking a zero tolerance against all forms of racism – structural and legislative – but also exercise high tolerance levels when approaching and encountering those that are culturally, religiously and ethnically different from you.

Being a non-racist is something quite different altogether. In this case, you can be tolerant and you generally teach your young children to be tolerant as well. But you do not necessarily act against those who deliberately or ignorantly practice racism against others, particularly minorities with whom, in your everyday life, you may have little to no contact, whether circumstantial or deliberate.

What Mandela said About the Children

But to be an anti-racist does mean that you have to actively seek out to engage with others who are culturally and ethnically different from you, over and above actively opposing racial discrimination.

The next chapter will explore the necessity for as well as benefits of cultural diversity. This book's opening anecdote made reference to Nelson Mandela's ideological stance. It is valid in the context of this chapter.

The argument goes that inherently, no single person is born a racist. In order to become a racist, a child would have to be taught. This does not necessarily entail structural classroom lessons as was the case during the National Socialism years in Germany in which anti-Semitism was very much part of the classroom's core curricula.

Do you Leave it Up to the Teacher?

Today, it could very well be argued that lessons on racism as well as anti-racism should be taught in school classrooms. There is clear evidence that, with notable exceptions, this is not being done in mainstream American as well as South African classrooms.

An important part of the anti-racism classroom perspective means having to revisit history textbooks for starters. Colleges and universities, on the other hand, have already gone far in redressing perceptions on colonisation and colonialism in which the colonist and colonialist was hailed while the continent's native or indigenous populations were regarded as inferior or 'savage'.

But teaching alt-history if you will does have its challenges in the sense that much of the country's indigenous history remains unrecorded (in writing) and confined to (unreliable) oral accounts.

Examining the School's Curriculum

A proactive anti-racist parent simply cannot leave it up to his or her child's teacher/s at this point in time. The teacher remains obligated to his or her school's core curricula. At the same time, it is still possible to subvert and intervene.

Ant-racism parents should have opportunities to speak out at their children's school board or parent/teacher meetings in which they make the clarion call to diversify the school's cultural history texts.

This, however, remains challenging when the anti-racism parent is in the minority. While it would be sad to do so, it may be necessary. To remove the child from a school that is clearly racially hegemonic.

The Issue of Demographics

And re-enrol that child in a school where the demographical pattern is more equitable. In such a case, it becomes easier for a young child to become accustomed to other children who are culturally and racially different.

Because without any form of indoctrination and with clear encouragement, but not forced, children will willingly mix as

playmates. But the issue of demographics remains challenging in the sense that schools are, by and large, located within areas that are already culturally, racially and socio-economically segregated.

The county's best schools are generally located in those areas that are middle to upper class and predominantly white.

Do you Encourage your Children to Fraternize with the Other

And the areas' worst schools are generally located in suburbs that are poor and underdeveloped.

These are also areas where mostly black American families will be housed.

This, of course, does make fraternization with the other challenging. How to overcome this? If it is not possible to relocate a child in a school that is culturally and/or racially diverse, it may still be possible to allow the child to engage other areas both public and private.

These could be sports clubs and public libraries, for instance.

The question, however, has been answered. As an anti-racism parent, it stands to good reason that you will be encouraging your child to fraternize with the other.

About Racism – The Kindergarten View

In an earlier chapter on reorienting conversations about racism, you were introduced to the importance of being a good listener.

This characteristic has always been an important one in the book of good parenting. Being able to listen to children as young as five years of age is critical.

It is at such points that an active parent should be able to make interventions and guide his or her child on a proper path. Exposure to a non-diverse school playground could pave the way towards feelings of inferiority if the child is in the minority.

The child needs to be taught his or her self-worth.

How to Respond to Children's Questions

And should you and your child be in the racial majority, it goes without saying that, as an anti-racist, you should be teaching your child to be culturally and racially tolerant and accepting at the earliest possible opportunity.

Regard this matter with the same seriousness you would when introducing your child to your family's spiritual or religious beliefs and/or practices.

Being exposed in the playground, the child is inevitably going to have questions. He or she should be allowed to ask these unashamedly, even if it may cause some embarrassment or discomfort to you. But then again, as a practicing anti-racist, and believer, there should be no shame.

Books & TV

Only pride.

Be proud that your child has the freedom to ask what may have been challenging questions. For children as young as four or five, such questions are usually direct, blunt and even to the point.

Such as;

'Why is John's skin so dark?' Or; why is Sarah's nose so big. Even; why does Richard look so pale. Is he sick?

These are the sort of questions young children may be prompted to ask. The best way to respond to them is to be as honest as possible. It is by far better for your young child to hear correct and truthful answers from you.

Conclusion

If you disincline your child, he or she will invariably approach other adults, the school teacher for instance, and the response may not always be desirable.

Finally, at that young age, its extremely necessary for you to monitor your children's TV watching and book reading activities. But at the same time, you should not shelter your child from the realities of this world.

Such realities will inevitably include having to encounter and deal with racism. Being a good parent has never been easy. And being a practicing ant-racist in this day and age certainly will not be easy either.

But, practice makes perfect. And as far as young children go, practicing what you preach may well make their early childhood development a little easier.

Chapter 13

Necessity of Diversity

Introduction

We have now reached the final chapter in this book on racism and white fragility. What follows thereafter will be a brief recap of what you have read and one final anecdotal motivation to spur you on in your effort to become racially-sensitive, perhaps even a practicing anti-racist.

The journey towards such ideals should become easier for you and your family if you are able to embrace what is known as cultural diversity. But in order to appreciate the need, first try and understand what it entails.

Becoming culturally diverse remains challenging for many, no matter which side of the cultural divide they are.

What is Diversity?

Why is this?

It could be that they are quite comfortable in their own skin but find it difficult to adjust to the social mores of others in which case they share little or no interest in foreign cultural habits and customs. And it becomes frustrating at times when others are not fully able to appreciate what they may be going through or have an interest in.

Another reason could be that they do not understand and know enough of their own culture. In order to embrace the other, they would first have to embrace themselves. And in order to do this, they would need to know themselves.

Why is Diversity Necessary?

If you are able to learn and understand your own cultural background, you will have a better chance of learning, understanding and appreciating other cultures.

The definition of diversity stems from the word divers – which refers to things, people, places, and cultures that are different. Diversity relates to being different or even adding variety to your personal or cultural life, as well as your socio-economic circumstances.

Sometimes diversity is forced upon us, but it often works better if (cultural) diversity is voluntary. In this sense the challenge remains. Because no one can be forced to accept or embrace one or many who are different.

Love can Build a Bridge

But it is being argued that cultural diversity is necessary. Presently there are far too many cultural and socio-economic conflicts within multitudes of communities across the country. Stark divides remain between the haves and the have nots.

It is the old story of the railway line. Across the tracks is a well-bred and prosperous community.

But in the opposite direction lie clusters of those mired in poverty. Apart from them being predominantly black American, they are also Asian, Latin American and even African.

The phenomenon of white fragility persists in the sense that a reluctance to share cultural and/or socio-economic resources with others persists.

Cultural Diversity

But at this point in time, economic, academic and scientific research is proving that there is now a definitive need for cultural diversity in all walks of life.

Mainly white racial hegemonies continue to resist this need, little knowing or accepting how this resistance to cultural change and acceptance is going to negatively impact on their own lives. It has been proven that the country will not be able to thrive economically if there is no cultural acceptance.

Today, owing to improved living standards and higher education levels, affluent white communities are rearing smaller families than in the past. And migrants seeking better economic opportunities also bring with them, let's just say, a diversity but breadth of skills now lacking in the country.

But before you Diversify; How well do you Know your Own Culture

Owing to the COVID-19 pandemic, forced and voluntary cultural and economic migration has been put on hold. But once all dangers have passed, it is only a matter of time before the drive towards a more culturally diverse society continues.

While life, cultural and/or economic, appears to be on hold for the time being, why don't you invest some time in getting to know your own culture? The further you delve into your family roots, from one generation to the next, the more surprising some of those results may become.

One of the surprises is that you may well find that you have something in common with others who are culturally, even racially, different from you.

Do Your Research Before Accepting An Invitation

These commonalities, however, do not have to be direct. They are usually general or subtle. And yes, they could even be related to seemingly trivial matters that we often take for granted. Like a preference for spicy food, perhaps.

Speaking of which; accepting a dinner invitation from a neighboring family that is culturally, religiously and racially different from yours could present you with a superb learning opportunity. Let's take this as a good example.

When accepting a dinner invitation, it may well be culturally expected of you to bring a bottle of wine. But what if your hosts are Muslim?

Learning to Be Comfortable in your Own Skin

You would need to know about the devout Muslim's strict intolerance to the consumption of alcohol. There are so manner other matters to do with cultural etiquette well worth pursuing. You may not have access to public libraries during COVID-19-related restrictions, but you still have access to the internet to carry out your research.

It is also important to learn how to stave off feelings of (racial) superiority or inferiority. While doing that, you are still able to embrace yourself and be proud of your cultural identity. But the challenge remains. This could best be served as a question to you right now. Do you not think that the time is rife to stop thinking of people in terms of their racial classification?

Learning to Love the Other

Is the preoccupation with race, not so much an awareness of it, not racial or even racist? Is it not possible to think in terms of the other by way of how he or she treats you rather? But more importantly, whether you are black or white, do you not think it is better to address your own self-worth before embarking on such preoccupations.

Two famous folk ballads are well worth quoting at this point in time. An earlier section heading made reference to Love Can Build A Bridge. There is also the famous jazz crooner, George Benson's enduring The Greatest Love of All.

Know the Difference Between Love and Like (And Dislike)

Indeed, in the song he suggests quite clearly that the ability to love yourself, no matter what, is the greatest love of all. And if you are able to do that, it surely becomes easier for you to embrace and love others.

And while there are those who quite literally aspire to building walls to keep others out, the very notion of love could be utilized to build a bridge, a bridge that erases current cultural divides. What do you think of this notion?

Finally, let's address the issue of racial sensitivity. It is to be made clearly understood that if person A does not like person B, it does not necessarily mean that he or she is bereft of love or even racist.

Rich Benefits of Cultural Diversity

This matter needs to be made clearly understood to those who may be racially sensitive. Perhaps the same could be said for those who are gender sensitive. And bear this in mind that if you are in the majority, you could be able to make reassurances to the other who may still feel threatened or inferior.

To dislike another is human. But that does not mean that there is hate or racial/racist intentions.

Finally, let's begin to explore the rich benefits of being culturally diverse. Perhaps without even realizing it, many of you are experiencing this today. The dinner table analogy is perhaps one of the best examples to utilize here.

Conclusion

You cannot deny that most of you enjoy pasta and pizza. That means you are enjoying something that is an important part of Italian culture. And did you know that your famous burger, fries and onion rings is not at all American.

It is both German and French. And those of you who have a refined taste for hot and spicy curries may be indulging in one of the many versions of the Indian sub-continent's cultures. Or for that matter, one of the many cultures across Southeast Asia.

There is certainly richness in diversity. Would life not be more interesting for you and your families if you were not culturally diverse?

Summarized Review of Book

In summarizing this book for you, let's run through a few of the book's highlights.

In order to understand and appreciate concepts from human life, it remains necessary to make reference to history. The old adage prevails in the sense that it is possible to learn from the past in an effort to either avoid repeating past errors and/or addressing current social ills; in this case, racism.

While in most cases, racism is no longer legislated, it remains, by and large, structural. The opening chapters of this book sought to briefly explore the origins of both legislative and structural racism.

Alongside of that, it was necessary to examine notions of white privilege and endeavor to understand where racial majorities' rage comes from. Part of examining the historical origins of racism in this country, turns out to be inspirational as well.

Why is this?

Well, inasmuch that racism was and remains brutal to many, the silver lining is that while racism still prevails today, it is not nearly as bad as it was in the beginning. It is fair to suggest that none of the change, progress and reforms you see today would have occurred had it not been for the sacrifices made and resilience of those who fought the struggle.

Without fear or favor? Hardly. It was never an easy fight because for much of the time, your champions of liberty, equality and fraternity were outnumbered and overpowered.

While the indigenous populations were decimated and/or annihilated by the colonizers who used what locals would refer to as 'fire-sticks' and worse, the colonizing masters perennially sought to weaken those that they enslaved.

And here too, there is irony in the history. This is perhaps why you have what is known as white fragility today. Many of today's whites, if they are not frustrated or put off by the 'behavior' of 'non-white' Americans and foreign migrants, they feel threatened.

It was already pointed out that affluent white American families are having fewer children. Also note that at some stage in the future, futurologists at large predict that the Hispanic population of the country could very well constitute the country's racial majority.

The fact that a majority of black Americans remain marginalized as a racial minority is owing to their poor economic and socio-economic conditions. An earlier chapter of Racism & White Fragility has pointed out what an impact racism, in any form, can have on people's health.

The consequences of being threatened and victimized by racism affects the physical and psychological health of those who are oppressed. And for generations now, many black Americans have been made to feel inferior to their white counterparts.

But there have always been those who have been able to escape this indoctrinatory mind-set, this book relates to the toxic mind-set. These black men and women have been able to proceed in life undeterred by racist taunts and suggestions of inferiority.

They have been to college, and more. They have made names for themselves in the professions. Indeed, whites would argue that progress made in behalf of many professional black Americans is due to legislated affirmative action. But they quickly forget the country's demographic circumstances.

And they do not so much mind their own structural practices, seeking always to put the native in his place, as a nineteenth to twentieth century British colonial colloquialism would have you know. Indeed, many professionals across the color bar, as well as those classified as physically challenged and forming part of sexual or gender minorities have benefited.

But many more have benefited through their own behavior. Perhaps for the purposes of inspiring the reader, this book could close with a classic but real life example. Meet Barack Hussein Obama, a native- born Hawaiian. And at the same time, meet Janet Mock, native-born Hawaiian.

Mr. Obama is the former president of the United States of America. He is also the first black American student to be elected president of the Harvard Law Society. During his two-term tenure, Mr. Obama sought to legislate for reforms in favor of racial, ethnic and cultural minorities across the board.

It would appear that the President led by example, given the composition of his multi-ethnic and multicultural cabinet, ranging from a white elder statesman to a transgendered female representative.

Speaking of which, Janet Mock is by now a world-wide celebrity of Hollywood proportions. Her claim to fame? Telling her own rags to riches story of how she was able to become the woman she was meant to be. Ms. Mock did not have the advantage of affirmative action.

No doubt that not only did she have to endure racial oppression, she would have had to put up with sexual and gender prejudice as well. How would you define Ms. Mock and Mr. Obama? Is it possible to classify Ms. Mock as an anti-racist in terms of her behavior and actions?

And in view of Mr. Obama's public position, would it be fair to suggest that, still to this day, he serves the interests of his country and beyond as a non-racist rather than an anti-racist? These are not open-ended questions but are designed to test your own resolve and intellect, perhaps even your conscience.

Indeed, it is not always possible for you to act in your own personal interests. All across the country, community-oriented circumstances, while they may be universal, they will always have their differences. Thankfully, and certainly in the interests of peace and harmony, it may not always be necessary to become an anti-racist.

But in numerous other instances, particularly in urban and congested centers across the country, the anti-racist stance remains necessary. It is as the late Nation of Islam leader once said;

Or is it? While this book has sought to inform, educate and guide you, the reader, is has never sought to indoctrinate you. You, the reader, are left with the final choice to make. How to contribute towards reversing the trends of racism in society and creating a better, more harmonious and productive society, creating a better tomorrow for your children, whom you will have taught.

www.ingramcontent.com/pod-product-compliance
Lightning Source LLC
Chambersburg PA
CBHW070052120526
44588CB00033B/1411